NATIONAL GEOGRAPHIC | **GLOBAL ISSUES**

T0069854

MIGRATION

Andrew J. Milson, Ph.D.
Content Consultant
University of Texas at Arlington

Acknowledgments

Grateful acknowledgment is given to the authors, artists, photographers, museums, publishers, and agents for permission to reprint copyrighted material. Every effort has been made to secure the appropriate permission. If any omissions have been made or if corrections are required, please contact the Publisher.

Instructional Consultant: Christopher Johnson, Evanston, Illinois

Teacher Reviewer: Andrea Wallenbeck, Exploris Middle School, Raleigh, North Carolina

Photographic Credits

Front Cover, Inside Front Cover, Title Page ©les polders/Alamy. **3** (bg) ©Santokh Kochar/Photodisc/Getty Images. **4** (bg) ©Danny Lehman/Corbis. **6** (bg) ©dbtravel/dbimages/Alamy. **8** (bg) Mapping Specialists. **10** (bg) ©Suzanne DeChillo/The New York Times/Redux. **12** (tr) Augustus F. Sherman. **13** (bg) ©philipus/Alamy. **14** (t) ©REUTERS/Lucas Jackson. **16** (bg) ©Pawel Libera/Corbis. **18** (t) Mapping Specialists. **19** (t) ©Mark Bryan Makela/In Pictures/Corbis. **21** (bg) ©Stuart MacFarlane/Arsenal FC via Getty Images. **22** (bg) ©Mark Thiessen/National Geographic Stock. **25** (bg) ©David Evans. **27** (t) ©Blaine Harrington III/Corbis. **28** (tr) ©Radius Images/Getty Images. **30** (br) ©Anthony Bradshaw/Photodisc/Getty Images. (tr) ©Pawel Libera/Corbis. **31** (bg) ©Santokh Kochar/Photodisc/Getty Images. (tr) ©Keenpress/National Geographic Stock. (br) ©Stuart MacFarlane/Arsenal FC via Getty Images. (bc) ©dbtravel/dbimages/Alamy.

MetaMetrics® and the MetaMetrics logo and tagline are trademarks of MetaMetrics, Inc., and are registered in the United States and abroad. The trademarks and names of other companies and products mentioned herein are the property of their respective owners. Copyright © 2010 MetaMetrics, Inc. All rights reserved.

For permission to use material from this text or product, submit all requests online at www.cengage.com/permissions.

Further permissions questions can be emailed to permissionrequest@cengage.com.

Visit National Geographic Learning online at www.NGSP.com.

Visit our corporate website at www.cengage.com.

ISBN: 978-07362-97707

Printed in Mexico
Print Number: 05   Print Year: 2023

INTRODUCING THE ISSUE
People on the Move... **4**

WORLD HOT SPOTS MAP
Centers of Migration... **8**

CASE STUDY ONE
NORTH AMERICA
New York: A Gateway City... **10**

CASE STUDY TWO
EUROPE
London: Many Nations, One City.................................. **16**

NATIONAL
GEOGRAPHIC **AT WORK**
SPENCER WELLS
Tracking Migration Through DNA.................................. **22**

WHAT CAN I DO?
Stage a Culture Fair.. **26**

RESEARCH & WRITE: NARRATIVE
COMMON CORE STANDARDS
Write a Narrative.. **28**

VISUAL GLOSSARY **30**

INDEX **32**

PEOPLE ON THE MOVE

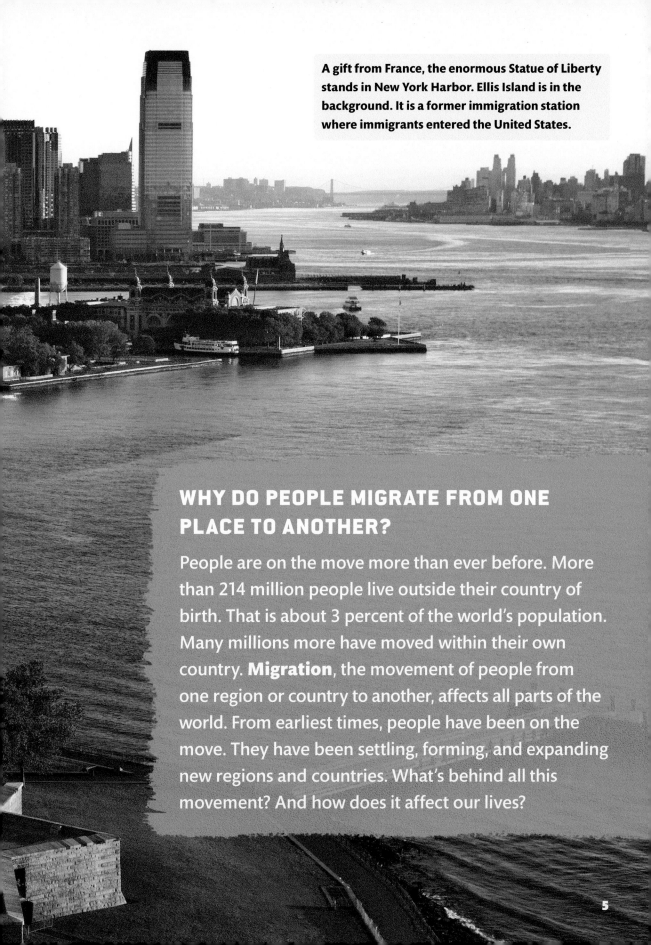

A gift from France, the enormous Statue of Liberty stands in New York Harbor. Ellis Island is in the background. It is a former immigration station where immigrants entered the United States.

WHY DO PEOPLE MIGRATE FROM ONE PLACE TO ANOTHER?

People are on the move more than ever before. More than 214 million people live outside their country of birth. That is about 3 percent of the world's population. Many millions more have moved within their own country. **Migration**, the movement of people from one region or country to another, affects all parts of the world. From earliest times, people have been on the move. They have been settling, forming, and expanding new regions and countries. What's behind all this movement? And how does it affect our lives?

STARTING OVER

Migrants are people who move from one region or country to another. **Immigrants** are people who move specifically to a new country. Some immigrants are unskilled workers. Others are scientists, doctors, engineers, teachers, and students.

Why would people leave their home country to begin life in a new place? Geographers often use the theory of push-pull factors to explain the reasons for migration. Push factors are conditions that *drive people away* from an area. Push factors include a low standard of living or war. Pull factors are conditions that *attract people to* a new area. Pull factors include high-paying jobs and good schools.

Changi Airport in Singapore is a major center of activity for immigration in Southeast Asia. Centrally located, the airport handles regional traffic as well as overseas flights.

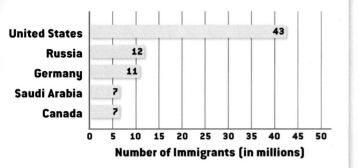

COUNTRIES WITH MOST IMMIGRANTS

United States — 43
Russia — 12
Germany — 11
Saudi Arabia — 7
Canada — 7

Number of Immigrants (in millions)
0   5   10   15   20   25   30   35   40   45   50

Source: Migration Policy Institute, 2010

GATEWAYS TO MIGRATION

The main reason people move is to find jobs. So it makes sense that most international migration is made up of people moving from poorer countries to wealthier countries.

The majority of immigrants settle in cities and suburbs where both skilled and unskilled workers are needed. Cities that attract large numbers of immigrants are called **gateway cities**.

Immigrants contribute to a gateway city by performing necessary jobs and by paying taxes. Immigrants also pay rent, buy homes, and purchase goods. All that spending feeds the local economy. Immigrants often revive city neighborhoods by starting new businesses and restoring old buildings. They also make cultural contributions. Residents of a gateway city might listen to reggae music from Jamaica, eat Vietnamese spring rolls, or watch baseball players from the Dominican Republic.

CHALLENGES AND REWARDS OF MIGRATION

At age 12, Luincys Fernandez (fer-NAN-dez) migrated to the United States from the Dominican Republic. She recalls her struggle to learn English in school: "I became mute. I just listened and listened and I couldn't figure it out, not even a word of what they were saying." Learning a new language is just one challenge immigrants face. You'll find out more about the challenges—and rewards—of migration as you read about two cities with large immigrant populations: New York City in the United States and London in the United Kingdom.

Explore the Issue

1. **Analyze Causes** What are some push-pull factors that lead people to migrate?

2. **Make Inferences** Why might the United States attract many immigrants?

Centers of Mig

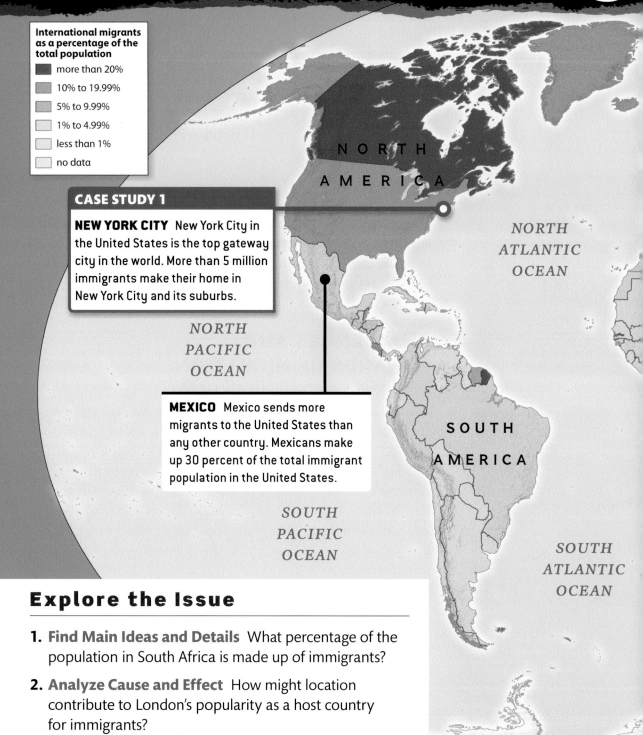

International migrants as a percentage of the total population

- ■ more than 20%
- ■ 10% to 19.99%
- ■ 5% to 9.99%
- □ 1% to 4.99%
- □ less than 1%
- □ no data

CASE STUDY 1

NEW YORK CITY New York City in the United States is the top gateway city in the world. More than 5 million immigrants make their home in New York City and its suburbs.

NORTH AMERICA

NORTH ATLANTIC OCEAN

NORTH PACIFIC OCEAN

MEXICO Mexico sends more migrants to the United States than any other country. Mexicans make up 30 percent of the total immigrant population in the United States.

SOUTH AMERICA

SOUTH PACIFIC OCEAN

SOUTH ATLANTIC OCEAN

Explore the Issue

1. **Find Main Ideas and Details** What percentage of the population in South Africa is made up of immigrants?

2. **Analyze Cause and Effect** How might location contribute to London's popularity as a host country for immigrants?

ation

Study the map below to learn about places that have been greatly affected by migration.

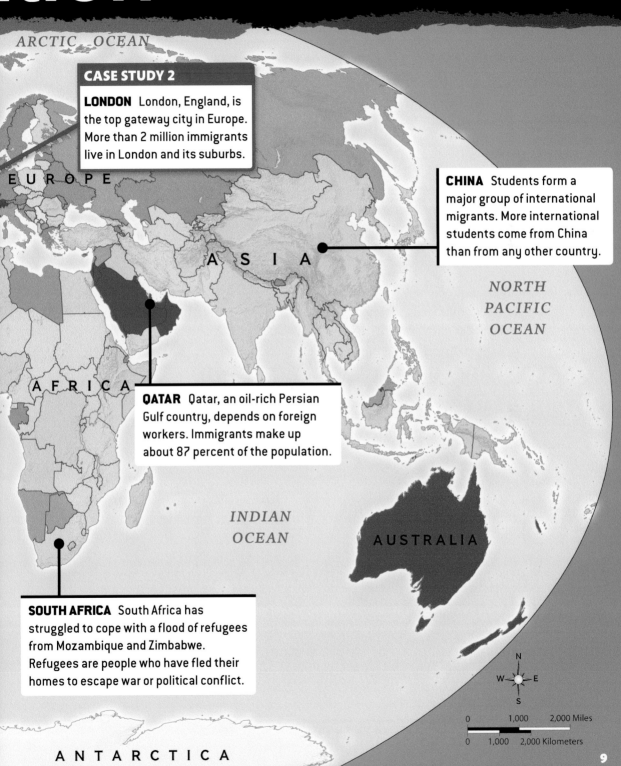

ARCTIC OCEAN

CASE STUDY 2

LONDON London, England, is the top gateway city in Europe. More than 2 million immigrants live in London and its suburbs.

EUROPE

ASIA

AFRICA

CHINA Students form a major group of international migrants. More international students come from China than from any other country.

NORTH PACIFIC OCEAN

QATAR Qatar, an oil-rich Persian Gulf country, depends on foreign workers. Immigrants make up about 87 percent of the population.

INDIAN OCEAN

AUSTRALIA

SOUTH AFRICA South Africa has struggled to cope with a flood of refugees from Mozambique and Zimbabwe. Refugees are people who have fled their homes to escape war or political conflict.

ANTARCTICA

| 0 | 1,000 | 2,000 Miles |
| 0 | 1,000 | 2,000 Kilometers |

Refugees from the rural plains of Bhutan now make their home in this apartment building in New York City.

NEW YORK
A Gateway City

A BEACON OF HOPE

One five-story apartment building in New York City houses a group of immigrants from rural Bhutan (BOO-tahn). They once lived in homes without electricity and plumbing. Bhutan is a small country in South Asia. These immigrants were originally from Nepal and were accused of entering Bhutan illegally. As a result, they were forced to leave Bhutan. Like millions of other immigrants, they came to New York City with little but hope for a chance at a better life.

New York City has provided hope to more immigrants than any other city in the world. It is the world's top gateway city. More than 5 million immigrants live in the metropolitan area of New York City. A **metropolitan area** includes a central city and its suburbs. In metropolitan New York City, immigrants make up almost 28 percent of the population. In the city itself, it's 37 percent.

A PATCHWORK QUILT

New York City's immigrants come from nearly every country in the world. This extraordinary **diversity**, or wide variety, in ethnic background is a hallmark of the city. Many immigrant groups have established their own neighborhoods within the city. The restaurants and other businesses reflect their ethnic background. Other neighborhoods have a wide mix of immigrant groups. In one elementary school in New York City, the students speak more than 35 languages.

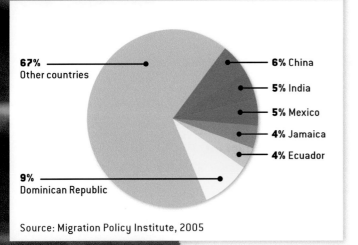

LARGEST IMMIGRANT GROUPS IN NEW YORK CITY

67% Other countries

6% China

5% India

5% Mexico

4% Jamaica

4% Ecuador

9% Dominican Republic

Source: Migration Policy Institute, 2005

This diversity in ethnic background is matched by the diversity in educational level and occupation. Some immigrants lack a high school education. Others have advanced degrees. Immigrants can be found in every occupation, including taxi drivers, doctors, nurses, accountants, and waiters. In addition, many students from other countries come to New York City for the educational opportunities. Students at the City University of New York come from more than 170 countries and speak more than 130 languages.

THE LURE OF THE CITY

A large part of New York City's appeal comes from its long history of welcoming immigrants. Ellis Island in New York Harbor was the busiest immigration station in the United States from 1892 to 1954. The station processed more than 12 million immigrants during that time. Historians estimate that almost half of all Americans have at least one ancestor who passed through Ellis Island. As immigrants neared the island, they saw the Statue of Liberty, a familiar symbol of the United States. To immigrants, the statue also represented the open arms of the city.

Another part of New York City's appeal comes from its standing as an international financial center and as home to the United Nations. As a result, the city draws highly educated foreign workers.

From 1892 to 1954 immigrants were screened for entry to the United States. The immigrants passed through the Registry Room, or Great Hall, on Ellis Island.

While New York City offers opportunities, it is an expensive place to live. Many immigrants end up moving from the central city to the suburbs or to smaller cities where the cost of living is lower.

A STEEP HILL TO CLIMB

Although New York City welcomes immigrants, their lives are not easy. Many live in crowded, rundown housing. The availability of jobs varies with ups and downs in the economy. Learning English can be a huge hurdle. Parents often end up relying on their children, who learn English in school, to guide them through life in an unfamiliar city.

Many immigrants not only support themselves but also send money called *remittances* to relatives in their home country.

Both government agencies and private organizations provide aid to immigrants in New York City. However, immigrants usually rely most heavily on one another. Relatives often share housing, meals, and job information. An experienced immigrant might help a newcomer learn to use the buses and train system. Immigrants often use informal ways like these to help people from their own country settle in a new place. This method of helping immigrants is known as **chain migration**.

Each year, almost 2 million people visit the historic Ellis Island Immigration Museum. The museum was reopened to the public on September 10, 1990.

BRINGING NEW ENERGY

Immigrants have had a huge economic impact on New York City. They have moved into neighborhoods vacated by residents who left for the suburbs. By establishing homes and opening businesses in vacant buildings, they have brought new life to dying neighborhoods. Their need for housing also has spurred new construction. Immigrants form a vital pool of workers for New York City, and they create jobs as well. Almost half of all small business owners in the city are immigrants.

Besides bringing energy to New York City's neighborhoods, immigrants have helped make the city a global powerhouse. Their connections to other countries contribute to globalization. **Globalization** is the linkage of the world's economies through international trade, communication, and migration. New York City is a key gateway for both foreign workers and global trade.

The cultural influence of immigrants is as great as their economic impact. New York's streets offer slices of life from all over the world.

New citizens celebrate after being sworn in during a naturalization ceremony in the Federal Hall National Memorial in New York City.

PLEDGING ALLEGIANCE

In order to immigrate to the United States legally, a person must obtain a **green card**—a permit that allows a foreigner to live and work in the United States permanently. The U.S. government issues a certain number of green cards each year, mainly to people with family connections or desired job skills.

Before applying for citizenship, a person must live in the United States for at least five years. An applicant then must demonstrate knowledge of English and of American history and government. More than 50 percent of the immigrants in New York City find a way to master the English language and acquire the knowledge needed to become citizens.

Explore the Issue

1. **Analyze Causes** Why does New York City attract so many immigrants?

2. **Form and Support Opinions** In your opinion, would limiting immigration help or hurt New York City's economy?

London

MANY NATIONS, ONE CITY

Vendors in London's scenic Leadenhall Market serve a variety of freshly prepared foods that immigrants have introduced into English society.

EMPIRE IN A CITY

Four young students sit around a table in a public school classroom in London. One student was born in India, another hails from Kenya, a third was born in Jamaica, and the fourth comes from Ireland. What do they all have in common? They were born in countries that were once part of the British Empire.

In the early 1900s, London was the capital of an empire that spanned the globe, making it one of the largest empires in history. An *empire* is a number of states under the control of one government. The empire no longer exists. However, people from countries once in the empire now migrate to London. In a way, it's as if the empire has moved to London.

London is the top gateway city in Europe. Its more than 2 million immigrants make up more than 30 percent of the city's population. Coming from nearly every country in the world, these immigrants make London the most diverse city in Europe. More than 300 languages are spoken in the city's schools.

In the last two decades, London has received a larger number of immigrants than ever before. During economic boom years, London welcomed foreign workers to fill job vacancies. But the global economic downturn of 2008 made it hard for many immigrants to find jobs. As a result, a large number returned home. Public debate about immigration has increased in London, along with economic concerns.

ARRIVING ON LONDON'S DOORSTEP

Almost 60 percent of London's immigrants come from former British territories overseas, such as India and Kenya. A large percentage also come from nearby countries in the European Union, especially Poland. The European Union is an economic and political partnership of European countries, to which the United Kingdom belongs. With some exceptions, citizens are free to migrate to any country within the European Union.

Many of London's immigrants moved away from their home countries because of low wages or a lack of jobs. Others, called **refugees**, left to escape war or political conflict in their home countries. For example, recent conflicts in the Mideast have led to a rise in the number of people from Libya and Syria seeking refuge in the United Kingdom.

17

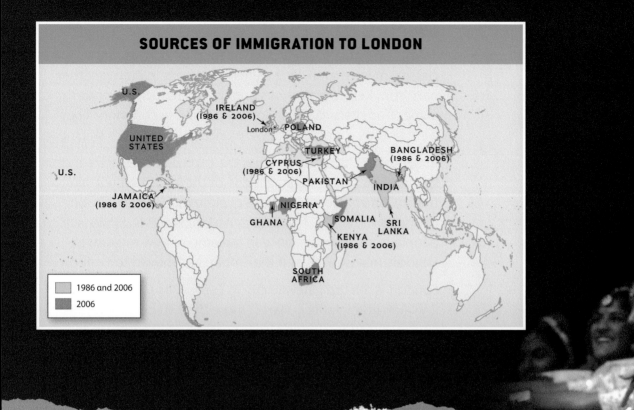

SOURCES OF IMMIGRATION TO LONDON

U.S.

IRELAND
(1986 & 2006)

London · POLAND

UNITED
STATES

TURKEY

BANGLADESH
(1986 & 2006)

U.S.

CYPRUS
(1986 & 2006)

PAKISTAN

INDIA

JAMAICA
(1986 & 2006)

NIGERIA

GHANA

SOMALIA

SRI
LANKA

KENYA
(1986 & 2006)

SOUTH
AFRICA

1986 and 2006
2006

ECONOMIC TUG

The biggest pull factor for immigrants to London is economic opportunity. Until the global economic downturn of 2008, London enjoyed a growing economy. The city offered jobs to workers at all skill levels, from scientists to housecleaners. **Guest workers** arrived from foreign countries to fill temporary, unskilled jobs. The British government also actively encouraged the immigration of highly skilled workers, such as doctors and computer specialists. Many came from wealthy countries, such as Australia and Germany. Some came to work in London for a few years to further their careers, with a plan to return to their home countries. Such **return migration** is common in the United Kingdom.

Another pull factor of London is its ethnic diversity. Immigrants can easily find communities of their own nationality in the city. Language is yet another pull factor. Many immigrants from former British territories and from the European Union know at least some English.

Dancers in London celebrate an important Indian holiday known as Diwali (di-WAH-lee), the festival of lights.

ADJUSTING TO A NEW LIFE

Like immigrants in other gateway cities, those in London face many challenges. Adam, a young Polish immigrant who speaks no English, found life in London extremely difficult. He explained, "There was no one I knew. It was a new environment. You can't speak to anyone." Due to a downturn at the factory where he worked, he lost his job. With no knowledge of English, he found it difficult to find other work. Adam ended up homeless, sleeping in parks and railway stations. He decided to return home to Poland in 2011.

Even immigrants with secure jobs often must settle for work that is below their skill level. An accountant, for instance, might work as a waiter. Many immigrants work long hours at low pay. Some not only struggle to support themselves, but they also try to send money home to their families. Adam, for example, sent money home to his mother, who supported six other family members. For many immigrants, the path to a middle-class life may take years, or even generations.

ENERGIZING THE CITY

The wide variety of its immigrant groups has made London as culturally diverse as New York City. Spread across metropolitan London are more than 50 different ethnic communities with their own shops and restaurants.

London's immigrant population has had a dramatic economic effect on the city as well. The number of immigrants in London jumped by more than 1 million between 1986 and 2006. This population growth brought a surge in demand for housing.

As immigrants moved in, they brought new life to deserted neighborhoods. They spurred redevelopment of old industrial areas of the city. Immigrants not only filled job vacancies, but they also created jobs by starting new businesses. London's growing economy attracted immigrants, and the immigrants helped the economy grow. However, that picture changed with the decline in the global economy in 2008.

PUBLIC CONCERN OVER IMMIGRATION

Although immigrants have helped boost London's economy, public concern about immigration is widespread. Some Londoners complain that the large number of immigrants make the city crowded. Many people claim that immigrants need to blend in more rather than stay in separate groups. In addition, the economic downturn raised concerns about the cost of providing social services to immigrants, especially refugees.

In response to public concerns, the British government has focused on reducing the number of refugees entering the country and on combating illegal immigration. *Illegal immigration* is settlement in a host country without official permission. The government also has placed a cap on the number of immigrants from outside the European Union. However, even with the policy changes, London remains attractive to immigrants.

Explore the Issue

1. **Summarize** How has immigration affected London?

2. **Compare and Contrast** How are London and New York City similar gateway cities?

Frenchman Thierry Henry wows his fans at London's Emirates Stadium. Thierry formerly played for the Arsenal football (soccer) team in London. He now plays for New York.

Tracking Migration Through DNA

WHERE DO WE COME FROM?

People have always wondered where they come from and how they got to where they are today. Research conducted in the 1980s provided support for a remarkable theory. Many human beings came from a group of African ancestors, some of whom began an incredible migration from Africa about 60,000 years ago. Eventually, their descendants spread out all over the world.

For decades, scientists have tried to piece together the story of human migration from fossils. But there are big gaps in the history. Now, scientists are opening a wider window on the past by analyzing DNA. **DNA** is the material in a cell that contains genetic information. A research project initiated by the National Geographic Society aims to chart the migratory history of human beings. The research project is known as the Genographic (jene-oh-GRAF-ik) Project. Scientists analyze the DNA of indigenous populations and the general public. When scientists find the same genetic marker in the DNA of two people, they can conclude that those two people share a common ancestor.

STUDYING GENETIC MAKEUP

Dr. Spencer Wells is a geneticist, author, and documentary filmmaker whose interest in biology and history began in childhood. Today, Wells is a National Geographic Explorer-in-Residence who heads the Genographic Project. He proudly describes the project as "a dream come true."

Wells has been on a fast track since his youth. He enrolled in college at age 16 and graduated three years later. While training at Stanford University's School of Medicine, he decided to focus his career on studying the genetic makeup of indigenous populations. Through field studies in which he gathered DNA for analysis, he began answering questions about early human migration. His studies formed the basis for his award-winning book and film *The Journey of Man: A Genetic Odyssey*.

The Genographic Project expands upon Wells's early field studies. Since the start of the project, Wells has traveled to more than 35 countries, including Chad, Tajikistan, Morocco, and Papua New Guinea.

WHAT DNA REVEALS

"The greatest history book ever written is the one hidden in our DNA," says Wells. Through the Genographic Project, Wells hopes to decode that language and reveal the history.

The Genographic Project began in 2005. It is a multiyear research effort with three parts. In one part, a team of international researchers collaborates with and collects DNA from groups of indigenous peoples around the world. In another part, the general public is invited to buy a Genographic Project Participation Kit and send in a DNA sample for analysis.

Scientists then use computers to analyze historical patterns in the DNA collected from both indigenous peoples and the general public. The scientists look for **genetic markers**, which are genetic changes that are distinctive in different populations of people. These markers can reveal the genetic groups that a person descended from—all the way back to a common African ancestor.

TRACING AN INDIVIDUAL'S MIGRATION

The third part of the Genographic Project involves the money raised from the sale of the Genographic Project kits. The money supports conservation work with traditional peoples and pays for additional project research.

Individuals who want to participate can purchase kits through the Genographic Project's Web site. They then send in a painless cheek-swab sample for analysis. The results show the migration paths that their ancient ancestors followed many thousands of years ago. They will even learn what percentages of their genome are associated with different parts of the world.

The results do not lead all the way to recent relatives, though. Individuals can learn about the recent migrations of their ancestors by interviewing parents and grandparents. Many people discover incredible migration stories of their own.

Explore the Issue

1. **Summarize** To which continent can all human beings trace their ancestry?

2. **Pose Questions** What questions do you have about the Genographic Project?

"The greatest history book ever written is the one hidden in our DNA."
—Spencer Wells

During an expedition to Chad, a country in north-central Africa, Wells visits local village leaders to explain the Genographic Project.

What Can I DO?

Stage a Culture Fair

How much do you know about the native cultures of immigrants in the United States? Find out more about the culture of one group, and use what you have learned to prepare a presentation. Then work with your classmates to stage a culture fair in your school to celebrate cultural diversity.

DISCUSS

- Conduct a class discussion and create a list of immigrant groups to feature in a culture fair. Your list should include as many different groups as possible.

- Form pairs and choose one immigrant group to research.

- Decide what kind of presentation you want to create, such as a poster or a multimedia slide show.

RESEARCH

- Use the Internet and library to research your immigrant group. Look at the census data for your city or state to see what immigrant populations live in your area.

- Find out about the language, customs, music, foods, and other features of the group's culture.

- Learn about the group's migration paths around the world.

Wearing costumes, Irish step dancers perform during a St. Patrick's Day parade in Denver, Colorado. Dancers must hold their arms straight down as they perform complicated steps.

CREATE

- Brainstorm titles for your presentation and sketch a layout.

- Write the text and find or create visuals for your presentation.

- Determine what other items to include in your presentation. For example, you might include a map, samples of food, a recording of music, or a dance demonstration. You may wish to include written or spoken language of the culture represented.

SHARE

- Work with your teacher to schedule a time for a schoolwide culture fair to share presentations.

- Take photos or digitally record the presentation as a record of your work.

- Conduct a class discussion on this question: What aspects of other cultures do you find most interesting? Why?

Research & WRITE
Narrative

Write a Narrative

What's it like to migrate to a foreign country where you don't speak the language? What happens on the first day of school or when you go to a store? Interview a classmate, relative, or acquaintance who is an immigrant. Use what you learn in the interview to write a narrative about the migration experience.

RESEARCH

Identify someone who relocated to your community from another country, and request permission to write about his or her experience.

- Make a list of questions, and schedule a time to interview the person.
- Record your conversation or take notes.

If you're an immigrant, you might write about your own experience.

DRAFT

Use your recording or notes to plan the narrative.

- As you draft the first paragraph, establish the context and point of view and introduce the narrator.
- In the body paragraphs, create dialogue and use description to develop the experiences or events.
- As you write, use transition words and phrases, such as *before*, *finally*, and *the next time*. These words tell your readers the order of events.
- Write a conclusion that follows from and reflects on the immigrant experience.

REVISE & EDIT

Review your draft to make sure your writing is clear.

- Did you explain the context and introduce the narrator?
- Do the events in your narrative follow a logical sequence?
- Does the dialogue help develop the experience? Do the details describe the experience clearly?
- Did you use a variety of transition words and phrases to convey the sequence of events and to signal shifts in time and setting?
- Have you included enough descriptive details and sensory language to capture the migration experience?

Revise the draft to improve the narrative flow. Then check the story for correct spelling, capitalization, and punctuation. Are ethnic names and places spelled correctly? Is the dialogue realistic? Do you conclude with your thoughts about the immigrant experience?

PUBLISH & PRESENT

Add a photograph or illustration to your narrative. Then create a booklet of migration narratives by combining your story with those of your classmates. As a class, decide on a title for the booklet, and ask a volunteer to design a cover. Share the printed booklet by reading the stories in class, or take turns bringing the booklet home for family members to read.

Visual GLOSSARY

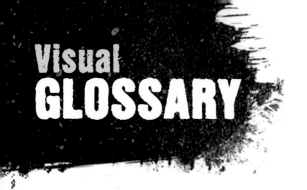

gateway city

chain migration *n.,* a way established migrants help others from their home country settle in a new place

diversity *n.,* a wide variety

DNA *n.,* the material in a cell that contains genetic information

gateway city *n.,* a city that attracts a large number of immigrants

genetic marker *n.,* a genetic change that is distinctive in different populations of people

globalization *n.,* the linkage of the world's economies through international trade, communication, and migration

green card *n.,* a permit that allows a foreigner to live and work in the United States permanently

guest worker *n.,* a foreigner who works temporarily in a host country

immigrant *n.,* a person who moves specifically to a new country

metropolitan area *n.,* a central city and its suburbs

migrant *n.,* a person who moves from one region or country to another

migration *n.,* the movement of people from one region or country to another

refugee *n.,* a person who leaves his or her home country to escape war or political conflict

return migration *n.,* movement back to one's home country

DNA

metropolitan area

immigrant

diversity

INDEX

British Empire, 17

Chad, Africa, 25
chain migration, 12, 30
Changi International Airport, 6
China, 9
cities
    appeal of, 12
    gateway, 7, 30
citizenship, 15
City University of New York, 11
cultural diversity, 17, 20
cultural fair project, 26-27
    see also diversity
cultural influence, 14

diversity, 11, 18, 30
DNA, 22-25, 30
    defined, 23

economic impact, 14, 20
Ellis Island, 4-5, 12-13
ethnic diversity, 17
ethnic neighborhoods, 11
European Union, 17, 18

gateway city/cities, 7, 17, 30
genetic marker, 24, 30
Genographic Project, 22-25
    process in, 24
Genographic Project
    Participation Kit, 24
global economic downturn,
    2008, 17, 18, 20
globalization, 14, 30
government
    aid to immigrants, 12
    and immigration, 18
green card, 15, 30
guest worker, 18, 30

Henry, Thierry, 21
housing, 14

illegal immigration, 20, 30
immigrant[s], 6, 30
    aid for, 12
    becoming citizens, 15
    cap on number of, 20
    challenges of, 19
    contributions of, 7
    countries with the most, 7
    energy of, 14, 20
    illegal, 20, 30
    in London, 17, 18, 20
    in New York City, 11, 12, 14
immigration
    illegal, 20, 30
    public concern about, 20
    see also migration

jobs, 6, 12, 14

language, 12, 19
    learning new, 7
Leadenhall Market, London, 16
London, 7, 8-9, 16-21
    as gateway city, 17
    concerns about immigrants in, 20
    effects of immigrants on, 20
    immigrant groups in, 17, 20
    sources of immigration to, 18

metropolitan area, 11, 30
Mexico, 8
migrant, 6, 30
migration, 30
    around the world, 8-9
    chain, 12, 30
    challenges of, 7
    personal stories, 24
    reasons for, 5, 6
    return, 18, 30
    rewards of, 7
    tracking with DNA, 22-25
    within European Union
        countries, 17
    see also immigration

National Geographic, 22-25
naturalization, 14-15
New York City, 4-5, 7, 10-15
    appeal of, 12
    as gateway city, 11
    immigrant groups in, 11
    impact of immigrants in, 14

push-pull factors, 6

Qatar, 9

refugee[s], 17, 30
remittances, 12
return migration, 18, 30

Singapore, 6
small businesses, 14, 20
social services, 20
South Africa, 9
Statue of Liberty, 4-5, 12
students, 11

*The Journey of Man: A Genetic
    Odyssey*, 23

United Nations, 12
United States, 8

Wells, Spencer, 22-25

SKILLS

analyze cause and effect, 8
analyze causes, 7, 15
compare and contrast, 20
create, 27
discuss, 26
draft, 29
find main ideas and details, 8
form and support opinions, 15
make inferences, 7
pose and answer questions, 24
publish & present, 29
research, 26, 28
revise & edit, 29
share, 27
stage a cultural fair, 26-27
summarize, 20, 24
write a narrative article, 28-29